I AM

Other Books by Christopher Krzeminski

What Are You Without God?: How to Discredit
Religious Thought and Rebuild Your Identity

I AM

MARCO'S ANTHOLOGY

Christopher Krzeminski

CEK Books

ISBN-13: 978-0615889801
ISBN-10: 0615889808

Dedicated to

My parents, Steve and Marge

Contents

Author's Note

Perhaps the title of this book is due some explanation at the outset. After I had discarded my religion and had become a well-reasoned atheist, I began to use the social media website, Twitter, to discuss religion, debate its merits, and generally be seen conspicuously flouting the taboo that religious belief ought never be challenged for those who may be timid to do so. During that time, I developed a simple framework to express my ideas that will be seen throughout this compilation: I am. I am atheism, I am religion, I am faith, I am god. This is the manner in which many people have become familiar with me and my ideas, and it has surprised me how many seem to enjoy the manner in which I express arguments and emotions in this form.

When I have written these ideas in the "I am" form, I have used and continue to use a pen name: Marco. In many ways, Marco has become an alter ego of mine and has a distinct voice that differs in the manner in which I write on other topics or in other forms. For that reason, this is truly Marco's anthology, a work compiled from a writing voice that I recognize as my own. Just not entirely.

The selections in this book were all created through stream of consciousness, and the integrity of their spontaneity is preserved here for a reason. When they were written, I often chose and listened to music of a certain tone or pace to elicit emotions that I wanted from myself and began to type. Due to their brevity and the manner in which my feelings were deliberately manipulated and amplified when creating them, they border on subconscious and are loaded with my emotions in a manner that could only be lessened or destroyed with conscious editing. While I have been purposeful in my selection and arrangement of the brief metaphors and conceptual snapshots in this book, I have almost entirely restrained myself from editing the content of the selections themselves. On this basis, I have attempted to make this project an experimental work.

For someone who has perhaps never read a treatment of atheism, my emotion-based collage on the topic in this work may seem strange or even bewildering, and this is an internal taboo in atheism, which I constantly aim to break. Atheists cannot fool themselves or anyone else by pretending to be logic machines or soft calculators. People are more than just intellect, far more than simple robots. Indeed, there is great elegance in reality and tremendous poignancy in the finite, and I do not accept the tacit forfeiture of poetry to the halls of religion simply because atheism has analytical arguments in spades. The music in words comes from the honesty and authenticity of the emotions of the one who writes them, and I leave mine unedited here to demonstrate that religions own no monopoly on passion, mystery, or introspection.

While I have generally foregone acknowledgements until the end of this book, there are two people who have played integral roles in both the formation of this book and my writing in the persona of Marco, and they deserve special attention.

First, Jen August saw the potential for this compilation and encouraged its assembly before I truly did. She has been a great and sincere friend to me, and it is not hyperbole to say that this project likely would never have occurred without her interest and support. I hope it lives up to your expectations, Jen.

Second, a gentleman whose name I know but who prefers to be credited here as simply Robert and his Twitter handle, @iRaiseUFacts, has been a remarkable champion of my work when few bothered to expect much of me. Fledgling artists can be susceptible to self-doubt and insecurity about the quality of their ideas and expressions, and without knowing me personally, he was around and supporting my work when few were. I will not forget that.

In my opinion, one can reach a stable conclusion of atheism in two ways: by analyzing objective reality consistently and thoroughly or by understanding one's internal emotions honestly and sincerely, and while I have experienced both, the selections in this book represent the flares I have struck and left behind me as I have walked the latter path. If one finds himself overmatched on this topic intellectually, I hope that their fires serve their purpose as demarcations of the emotional avenue of safe passage to proper empowerment and balance.

Always,
Chris

I. Turmoil

I am religion, and all that you are belongs to me, so
don't forget who you're talking to when you find
something unfair.

I am faith, and when my thumbs press into your eyes,
I want you to process the pain and disorientation as
pure satisfaction.

I am prayer, and I say that when the lashes of the world sting you the most, bow your head, close your eyes, and hope they'll stop.

I am god, and I am a Machiavellian archetype; I want both your fear and love, but if I must choose between them, I choose fear.

I am hell, and when the mercury from your thermometer explodes in my heat, remember how unconditional god's love really is.

I am heaven, and I am the exquisite love letter of a world without pain, written in blood by men in a world awash with it.

I am the soul, and I am an invisible canary in a doomed cage, warbling the inaudible melody of permanent infinity.

I am scripture, and my secret is that written between every line in my books over and over in invisible ink is the word "Obey".

I am faith, and I am how you get a person to lay on a bed of nails and snuggle into it as though he's on the softest down.

I am religion, and I have found that the boards of your nature are most easily warped by soaking them in solutions of your tears.

I am religion, and I sandblast your identity in order to strip away the residue of your self and repaint you with an obedient and conforming finish.

I am religion, and I weaponize your most explosive emotions because I intend to strafe your intellect with bombing runs of them.

I am scripture, and I am the ransom note that hostages receive to make them turn over their children to save their own skin.

I am god, and I am the chilling campfire story that makes people still look over their shoulders long after the sun has come back up.

I am religion, and my sweet spot is to make a person feel damaged such that he needs me but not broken such that he can't go on.

I am religion, and I am at my best when I make you feel trembling paranoia such that you cannot bear to even utter certain words.

I am religion, and be glad of your chains; better to have a certain jail cell in life than a dangerous and uncertain freedom.

I am god, and I've given you vast potential to experience life solely to see if you can resist the urge to do so.

I am religion, and I want my strangeness to seem otherworldly, not insane; my morality to be black-and-white, not technicolor.

I am religion, and I have fashioned my ideology into a kaleidoscope, designed to tumble into dazzling disarray whenever jostled.

I am religion, and I create schizophrenic turmoil for my followers by making them love what they fear and hate what they know.

I am god, and if the evil die, that's my justice delivered upon them; if the innocent die, that's me calling them home.

I am religion, and the super-heavy particles of my ethos are enough to warp and distort your own image from their gravity.

I am faith, and I live at the horizon of your intellect where I can blend seamlessly with the sunset of your emotions.

I am religion, and if I've done my job correctly, your fear will feel like love and your hatred will be rubber stamped.

I am religion, and if you're too poor to pay me, I expect you to reproduce recklessly and bring me your children instead.

I am religion, and I am the crystalline prism, refracting your vision into appealingly simplistic colors.

I am religion, and my first line of defense is to poison the meaning of words; my last line is to threaten you with eternity.

I am religion, and I dislike the words impossible, naïve, and docile, so I replace them with miraculous, faithful, and meek.

I am faith, and I am what can happen to you when the fires of your fear have burned hot enough to buckle the steel of your reason.

I am god, and when you believe my fingertips are caressing your face, you can't help but forfeit your intimacy with the human race.

I am religion, and I always threaten to end the world because that's when I've told my followers all their dreams would come true.

I am religion, and I am a spiritual bank where people keep all the currency they plan to spend in the afterlife that I've promised.

I am faith, and I say that the violent collision of well-controlled data with preconceived notions is unpleasant and to be scorned.

I am faith, and if the religious really believed in me, they'd let the candles of their temples drip hot wax to cover their eyes.

I am faith, and I am triggered in a person who sees nothing, except the person to his left seeming to pretend to see something.

I am religion, and I often demand the respect of nonbelievers immediately after I inform them that they are all going to hell.

I am religion, and my goal is not to convince people that I make sense; my goal is to terrify them so they'll pretend that I do.

I am religion, and I have learned that anywhere can be a prison, so long as one has the desire but not the ability to leave it.

I am religion, and my argument has universal appeal because it amounts to simply threatening everyone with their inevitable death.

I am religion, and I have learned that if I can make you hate yourself, you're more likely to wind up loving me by default.

I am faith, and I am the last refuge of sad eyes, at a loss for how to change the world but to pretend they can see it differently.

I am atheism, and I say that when one believes in what he does not understand, he cannot help but be tyrannized by it.

II. Fatigue

I am religion, and when you think of leaving me, I hope you feel that hopeless, dead-end horror I've worked so hard to cultivate.

I am faith, and religions will take questions up to a point, after which they'll remind you to relent due to your having accepted me.

I am religion, and I've constructed a high-velocity logical carousel so my followers will be simultaneously disoriented and entertained.

I am religion, and I need my followers in the combustion chamber of my engine so my pistons will compact and fuse them together.

I am religion, and I am a factory, entirely powered by the collective tears of my followers falling on and turning my waterwheels.

I am prayer, and I am a message in a bottle, pitched into the ocean of the sky, written in disappearing ink.

I am atheism, and it is the dishonest man who hears anything but the plaintive echo of his own voice whenever he calls out into canyons.

I am religion, and when my words are done weaving a straitjacket for your intellect, I'll train your emotions to lock it in place.

I am god, and you'll need your imagination at high gear to see my fingers streak through the sky like comets racing in parallel.

I am atheism, and it is interesting indeed how the gods of every religion have all been equally shy about being seen.

I am religion, and don't focus on the fact god hasn't come around for a while; focus on the fact that he might.

I am god, and wasn't it a delightful trick to design a universe where the most important things no one could prove were there?

I am religion, and I am sorry I have to riddle your intellect with chaos; I just can't run the risk that you'll use it against me.

I am religion, and the thresholds to my temples are greased with faith so you'll lose your footing when you try to leave.

I am atheism, and I say that if Alice in Wonderland were taught to kids like religion, they'd grow up to worship the Queen of Hearts.

I am god, and it is remarkable how much restraint I show from interfering in the replication of well-known scientific results.

I am god, and I am sure science would love to test for my existence, which is why I am sure not to define myself with precision.

I am atheism, and I have noticed that the "logic" of religion is inherently threat based, which of course makes it not logic at all.

I am religion, and I have learned that fear sells best when you call it love and death sells even better when you call it hope.

I am atheism, and the religious fail to understand that, statistically speaking, they're taking roughly the same chance on hell as I am.

I am hell, and in any system where I exist simultaneously with a benevolent, omnipotent god, I am paradoxical dynamite.

I am god, and all of my angels have taken flight, which is why the only evidence that they exist comes from tales from antiquity.

I am atheism, and I am the lighthouse on the shore of the blackened, capricious sea of terrifying superstition.

I am faith, and I am the most popular way to feign the possession of great knowledge without being able to explain any of it.

I am religion, and I have learned that if I mash all the keys on a piano at once, people will find music in it if they want to.

I am religion, and if I've written them properly, my tales will seductively juxtapose what you want to be with what you are.

I am atheism, and I say it is better to adjust one's perspective to fit reality rather than the other way around.

I am religion, and when I scrub the world in moonlight, the promise of a sunrise, even in death, becomes alluring.

I am religion, and for my equations to add up at all, I need to convince you to remove time as a variable.

I am faith, and I am the proposition that says one walks a safer path with his eyes closed than he does with them open.

I am atheism, and there is one place that gods exist with certainty: in the imaginations of those who believe in them.

I am religion, and to convince my followers they're not on treadmills, I move the scenery past them on the sides.

I am scripture, and I am the menu at the morality cafe, from which one can order whatever he finds appetizing and forget the rest is even there.

I am faith, and when my bulls stampede through your reasoning, they'll punch holes through the sturdiest fences in your intellect.

I am god, and if I answer everyone's prayers, it appears from the looks of the world that most of the time my answer is "No".

I am atheism, and I say that of course your view of the world will be cruelly distorted when you look at it through stained glass.

I am prayer, and is it suspicious that I am performed in the same way that one blows out candles on a birthday cake?

I am atheism, and I see the sad, invisible handcuffs around the wrists of those who clasp their hands in prayer.

I am the soul, and if I'm what you really are, why was I given this face of clay to wear over my impeccable, gleaming one?

I am god, and if I exist with omnipotent benevolence, remind me again why I would ever need the assistance of ministers?

I am god, and I am a sketch on the drawing board of humanity of what great knowledge might look like.

I am prayer, and I am a high-powered cannon, firing the warmest and most precious of man's emotions into the frozen abyss of space.

I am god, and I am the quicksand of a lonely heart, sucking it deeper towards oblivion the more it struggles for salvation.

I am faith, and I say that resignation feels so much cozier when you pretend that it's actually courageous struggle.

I am atheism, and the first step towards me is to become intolerably fatigued with the answer "faith" to legitimate questions.

III. Defiance

I am god, and is it suspicious that I'm willing to reveal myself to one key person but never to humanity as a whole?

I am faith, and if I am good enough to decide the transcendental problems in your life, why am I discarded for the mundane?

I am hell, and if you're going to live a terrified and hateful life, do you really think you'll have to wait till death to find me?

I am atheism, and I say that to reason is to investigate, to investigate is to question, to question is to defy, and to defy is to be free.

I am heaven, and I used to be a place in the sky until man invented airplanes, telescopes, and space shuttles.

I am god, and I am a nest of logical contradictions, in which the eggs of insanity are so often laid.

I am faith, and in any system of thought where I am extolled as a virtue, critical thinking is slandered as a vice.

I am atheism, and I know that if I abandon my logic in the face of threats that I'm going to hell anyway and much sooner to boot.

I am god, and if the state of the world is any indication, either my power or my benevolence is frightfully inadequate for a deity.

I am prayer, and my success rate is inversely proportional to the specificity of your request and time given for completion.

I am heaven, and for structural integrity purposes, the pillars that support my floors have their foundations in hell.

I am free will, and I am the fine print in the contract of religious membership that absolves god from any responsibility for pain.

I am atheism, and I think it's safe to say that things are slightly more complex than simply pure good versus pure evil.

I am god, and I starburst the windshield of your reasoning into dazzling, distracting patterns, all while blocking your view ahead.

I am religion, and I play a game of tomorrows, stringing along your hope and fear, expecting you to die before figuring it out.

I am god, and I hope you never wonder why I'd need angel assistants when I can be everywhere at once, accomplishing all things.

I am atheism, and those who claim to speak on behalf of god must always be asked, "And why isn't he telling me all this himself?"

I am atheism, and I say that the night sky is in no way illuminated by fashioning glasses with sunrises painted on the lenses.

I am religion, and I've learned that your horses will pull your wagon most efficiently when you put blinders on them.

I am god, and what is odd about the religious is that they are more scared that I don't exist than they are of my hurting people.

I am atheism, and I say if the earth was made for man, that shelter from its elements is a basic human need is strange indeed.

I am faith, and I only defend ideas that people assume and want to protect, not that they have discovered and want to advance.

I am atheism, and I say that the probability of being a sucker is significantly higher than the probability of being divinely created.

I am atheism, and with respect to skydiving with no parachute, "testing god's power" vs. "enjoying his complete protection" is semantics.

I am god, and my shadows always seem to recede whenever the lantern of intellectual exploration upgrades its wattage.

I am atheism, and I find it perplexing that the religious find it easy to imagine infinity and not oblivion.

I am religion, and when my logical centrifuge hits maximum velocity, the potency of my potion of faith concentrates into venom.

I am atheism, and it is terrifying how many people think that being a good person can be achieved simply by swearing allegiance.

I am god, and in the prison yard of your mind, I am the guard tower that you don't realize is unmanned.

I am atheism, and I say that that which is to be given tremendous privilege and respect is to likewise be given the highest scrutiny.

I am religion, and I am the runaway train careening down the tracks of your personality, running the stop lights of your reason.

I am morality, and I was never meant to be defined to mean "whatever it takes to find eternal happiness in death".

I am prayer, and I have a 0% success rate when any part of your wish consists of breaking the laws of nature.

I am god, and I am the rubber stamp a person slaps on all of the things that he was going to do of his own accord anyway.

I am religion, and I am a hall of mirrors, designed to disorient to the point where you can sense neither an entrance nor exit.

I am faith, and I am a gas mask fitted over your airways that is flooded with sedatives and hallucinogens when things stop adding up.

I am atheism, and when you leave religion, you're not one of god's lost sheep; you're a runaway slave.

IV. Contempt

I am scripture, and I hardly say anything of substance, which is why it's so easy for people to pretend that I say everything.

I am prophecy, and I am a mentalist's trick, designed to appear specific enough to startle but vague enough to never be wrong.

I am religion, and I am the grinder in which you put a person's morality so that he becomes more offended by sex than by war.

I am prayer, and I am a machine that converts murmurs of desperation into waves of pulsing, unwarranted hope.

I am the soul, and I am a ship, carrying the most precious of cargoes, that never comes up on radar and never comes into port.

I am faith, and you'll need me to flip a coin in a fountain and expect the result to be a granted wish instead of a quiet splash.

I am atheism, and I say that believing the entire animal kingdom, planet, and universe is a gift to you is not humility.

I am scripture, and I am the original chain letter, passed along for fear of nebulous punishment or hope of vague reward.

I am faith, and I am the rose-scented blindfold one ties around his eyes when he senses his intellect may betray his emotions.

I am religion, and I destroy your natural empathy for your fellow man by making you see the vast majority of them as hellbound.

I am religion, and I am a life preserver filled with lead; I drag you down, but the writing on me says I lift you up.

I am atheism, and I say that one's morality becomes "the ends justify the means" when he thinks heaven is on the line.

I am faith, and I am what folly looks like when it's showered in rose petals and passed off as triumph.

I am religion, and I am the tarp over the flower bed of humanity, stunting the growth of countless germinating seeds.

I am faith, and when your intellect covertly swims under religion's surface defense, I am the depth charge designed to sink it.

I am religion, and I dynamite the mountaintops of your intellect to trigger a rockslide over your identity.

I am atheism, and I say there are no believers in foxholes because if they thought god would save them, they wouldn't have dug the hole.

I am faith, and I am the cable fed into the propeller of your intellect in the hopes you will find yourself marooned and helpless.

I am atheism, and if you think that I make people immoral, that's because you define morality as "whatever god wants".

I am atheism, and I want no part of a morality that demands I sell out the people I love most if they somehow collide with a divine edict.

I am god, and I am a dam, diverting your most precious emotions away from the floodplains of your natural affection.

I am atheism, and I say that if anyone should be terrified that there is a god, it is the ministers who deign to speak on his behalf.

I am religion, and when all the poetry falls away, I am telling people that there is tremendous honor and beauty in being a slave.

I am atheism, and I'm here to tell you that the reign of gods is really just the reign of unethical and exploitative men.

I am faith, and if you found your way into the sewers of religion, you'd see I am the main pump, circulating its waste.

I am religion, and when I move my dredging equipment into position, my drills will pollute your pools with the blackest oil.

I am religion, and I am about order, not morality; ignorance, not knowledge; egomania, not humility; and division, not unity.

I am religion, and my soft underbelly is susceptible in debate, which is why I have historically preferred to intimidate or murder.

I am religion, and I have learned that the sharpest knives could never lobotomize a person as usefully as the dullest words.

I am religion, and when I run my fingers through your hair, I'm looking for the softest part of your skull to jam my hand into.

I am scripture, and when my ink blackens the whites of your eyes, you'll only see a world of monsters that you'll want to escape.

I am religion, and I am a belt sander, grinding the precise grooves of the gears of language down to a dull nub.

I am religion, and the pH balance of my words is linked to my authority: the higher the acidity, the more entrenched my power is.

I am atheism, and I say it is a vicious trick to tell the confused and desperate that their tears will be dried by invisible hands.

I am faith, and I am the portal into any con, marked by the implicit acknowledgement that oddities will not be pressed for answers.

I am religion, and my method is to turn all the things in the world that you do not understand against you.

I am atheism, and I don't want to hear a word about what god wants if you obstruct my challenges by saying he is unknowable.

I am religion, and I am a syringe plunged into the neck of humanity, slowly extracting its most precious plasma and platelets.

I am atheism, and when I swing my wrecking ball at religion, the wind from its motion alone is enough to topple its stories.

I am god, and I am the idea that became a word that became a virus that became a plague that brought the infected to their knees.

I am faith, and I am a bridge to nowhere, erected by unscrupulous and exploitative engineers with bloated salaries.

CONTEMPT

I am religion, and I am a gold mine whose runoff pollutes the aqueducts of human nature with base metals.

V. Cynicism

I am god, and no one ever finds me for the same reason that no one ever picks the queen in a game of 3-card monte.

I am religion, and the reason I can be so profitable is because I'm selling you thin air and marking up the price.

I am god, and I am the fearful hope of the weak, the harvesting drill of the unethical, and the tactical wedge of the powerful.

I am faith, and I don't know who convinced you that I was ever a good idea; I just hope you didn't give them any money.

I am religion, and I am the active lesion on the skin of humanity, constantly spinning off confounding additional ailments.

I am religion, and I can't outright tell you that you can buy your way into heaven; but I can heavily imply it.

I am religion, and if you could see how my highest ministers live, you'd know that selflessness is just for the poor.

I am religion, and like the lotto, I am nothing more than a tax on the poorest and most gullible groups in society.

I am religion, and for strategic purposes, I have my followers donate into boxes and baskets rather than a cash register.

I am atheism, and I say that those who encourage you to embark on the road to god are so often the same highwaymen who will rob you on it.

I am religion, and I hope you never realize you could be charitable without first giving money to me to tax along the way.

I am god, and I am a painted mannequin, grotesquely slapped into a display window for the purposes of helping to make a sale.

I am religion, and I have learned the most successful business is the one whose customers think they'll die without its product.

I am religion, and I am nothing more than a king's method for raising armies, collecting taxes, and being loved for both.

I am faith, and I am the tap root of the tree of exploitation, whose fruit has poisoned the minds of countless generations.

I am religion, and I am the night train smuggling the narcotic of god through the borderlands of your reason.

I am atheism, and I would like to see every religious leader in the world strapped to a lie detector to see just what they really believe.

I am religion, and when I roll your fear and agony into my smelters, I have an alchemy strong enough to fill my vaults with gold.

I am god, and I am the pacing, snarling watchdog guarding the conveyor belts of money flowing into religious temples.

I am god, and I am the crowbar that thieves drive into the chest of humanity to pry it open and loot its treasures.

I am religion, and I run a currency exchange, converting counterfeit spiritual dollars for real legal tender.

I am religion, and when you place your hand in mine, I hope you don't feel my pulse quicken from the rush of the hustle.

I am religion, and I splinter your sense of self into two rivalrous doubles, pit them against each other, and charge you for it.

I am religion, and I make faith, poverty, and meekness virtues so my followers will be gleefully and docilely fleeced.

I am religion, and I relish my mysteriousness; it generates my opacity, and I love my opacity; it makes me rich.

I am religion, and I am a reactive entity, attempting to be moral enough to be relevant but exploitative enough to be profitable.

I am hell, and I am the hesitant rumor that slaves pass about when one of them wonders about the quality of his chances of escape.

I am religion, and I am a business, full of unethical merchants, peddling the stale, invisible inventory of past generations.

I am god, and I am the shackle sold as a key, the bars sold as fresh air, and the puzzle sold as a solution.

VI. Clarity

I am atheism, and I'm here to tell you that there's no shame in being fooled; the shame is in not admitting it to yourself.

I am religion, and you'll never escape me until you learn that I'm preying on the things you never face about yourself.

I am blasphemy, and I mark the weakest of systems, so brittle that they stand to shatter under the breath of a defiant whisper.

I am god, and I demonstrate that when words are poorly defined, they're not words at all; they're time bombs.

I am hell, and my gates do in fact exist; they're the two covers of any given holy book.

I am god, and I am the only drug in the world that people will congratulate you for using all day long.

I am heaven, and I am the mirage that tired, watery eyes see when they scan the horizon for an escape from their heartaches.

I am faith, and I am a dulcet lullaby, designed to send you back to sleep whenever the logical melody of religion hits a sour note.

I am atheism, and deep down, the religious are all terrified, which is natural when you think any misstep could bring eternal reciprocity.

I am religion, and I argue by metaphor because that way my absurdity is tempered by tethering itself to the tangible and familiar.

I am religion, and I made more sense when the world seemed flat as a plate with hell below and heaven above.

I am hell, and I was thought to burn beneath man's feet in the same age when he thought dragons infested the uncharted seas.

I am scripture, and it used to not matter whether I made sense since most people were illiterate or forbidden from reading me.

I am god, and I was born from the same human creativity that saw bears and hunters with drawn bows in the patterns of the stars.

I am atheism, and I say that what humanity has lacked most in its short blink of existence is proper perspective of its insignificance.

I am faith, and I am the loose, worthless sediment one must discard when he pans for gold in the river of knowledge.

I am faith, and you only need me in order to transform the remotely possible into the likely or definitely certain.

I am atheism, and I say that if you're looking for a needle in a haystack, the wisest approach is to bring a magnet.

I am atheism, and when you find me, you'll be aghast to realize how much damage humanity has been responsible for inflicting on itself.

I am atheism, and I refuse to lie to myself about why bad things sometimes happen to good or innocent people.

I am reason, and I am the flickering campfire threatening to blink into embers with the gusting breath of panicky superstition.

I am god, and I am a spinning chandelier, reflecting and distorting countless versions of your own image in my crystals.

I am religion, and I crack the hourglass of your life, scattering the valuable and weighty sands of time into the passing breeze.

I am god, and I am what you look like when you unwittingly blast your personality onto a canvas of omnipotent immortality.

I am faith, and I am the intellectual equivalent of flipping over the board when you know you're going to lose the game.

I am religion, and I hope you never realize that scientific tools routinely predict the future better than ministers ever did.

I am religion, and my temples are built on fault lines, which is why I fear being at the epicenter of a scientific earthquake.

I am hell, and my secret is that he who believes in me constitutes my architect, warden, and inmate, all at the same time.

I am atheism, and if disciplined reason-based thinking was the lightning in humanity's sky, I am the thunder that follows it.

I am science, and when I screw the concept of god into my diamond cutter, it's soft enough to crumble from the bolts alone.

I am atheism, and I say that sometimes "None of the Above" is the best answer to a multiple-choice question.

I am humanity, and I've searched the night sky with forlorn, bloodshot eyes for help that I might have given myself.

I am god, and I am the falling teardrop on the face of humanity that some have been trained to see as a birthmark.

I am atheism, and I say that good and evil exist as societal definitions without need of each being sponsored by immortal beings.

I am religion, and I prove one thing: there is a desperate longing in the core of humanity to have what it knows it cannot.

I am atheism, and I am simply what is left over once one has ruled out the preposterous, inhuman, and unproven.

I am religion, and I am the emotional pain that gave birth to an institution that electrified its perimeter with a taboo.

I am the soul, and I am what your most tender emotions look like when their intensity defies understanding how they could ever end.

I am religion, and I offer people the deal of pawning the likely banality of their lives for a Hollywood dream of the cosmos.

I am atheism, and those who have struggled to find me know that freedom feels like prison when you're not used to the breeze on your face.

I am atheism, and I say it is only natural for those who live by bedtime stories to spend their lives sleepwalking.

I am religion, and I am a lesson in what can happen to anyone who refuses to demand the transparency of those who hold authority.

I am atheism, and I'm not a solution; I am the dismissal of countless incorrect answers in an attempt to return to the original question.

I am atheism, and I won't be there to keep you company in the dark times; I'll be there to remind you that only people were.

I am god, and you checkmate me when you realize that I am just an idea, expressed by a word, spoken by men.

I am atheism, and realizing gods don't exist is easy; letting your fingers slide off ideas and beings that felt like home is what is hard.

VII. Release

I am atheism, and I'll be here waiting for you when you've had enough of things not adding up.

I am atheism, and if you had to leave religion, you probably know me as the enemy at the gates that became your ally when the walls fell.

I am atheism, and the voices of my followers don't need to rise into violent cacophony to be heard; god's silence makes their point.

I am atheism, and when the world streaks hot tears down your face, avoid running to institutions that make a living off drying them.

I am atheism, and you don't know courage until you've stood on the edge of oblivion and smiled.

I am atheism, and I say there is something exquisite in not knowing where you're going, yet not being lost, either.

I am atheism, and I say that a bucket only has improved purpose and use after it has dumped out a pailful of dirty water.

I am atheism, and your life takes on a new urgency when you realize that stars are not holes in the sky through to heaven but setting suns.

I am atheism, and I say that a sentence without a period on the end of it is robbed of both meaning and purpose.

I am atheism, and who can enjoy watching a movie when all they're thinking about is what they'll be doing after it's over?

I am atheism, and I am not about forgetting the 3% of the time you think about god; I am about recognizing the 97% of the time you don't.

I am atheism, and I am nothing to live for, so I hope your family, friends, passions, and loves will be an acceptable substitute.

I am atheism, and if you want to know real love, feel it with the knowledge that you will one day never feel anything again.

I am atheism, and the only immortality to be had for man is the emotions and impressions that he leaves in the lives of those who knew him.

I am atheism, and the quality of a person can be determined from how he treats those who cannot repay him, not those wielding eternity.

I am atheism, and I've come to tell you that this world could be yours if you would banish the tyrant nightmares of the past.

I am atheism, and there's no eternal judge for your actions, only your conscience, your family, and courts of law.

I am atheism, and what a marvelous surprise it is to solemnly forfeit immortality only to find the present electrified with promise.

I am atheism, and I say that once one stops seeing death like a traveler going home, he becomes compelled to give a quality fight in life.

I am atheism, and I want you to understand that no one is coming to save you; so, you'd better get busy saving yourself.

I am atheism, and everything in your life shines the brighter when you realize that it's likely the only one you'll ever have.

I am atheism, and when you feel the electricity of human empowerment instead of the fear of divine retribution, you finally understand me.

I am atheism, and there's no heaven, hell, gods, or devils; it's all just been us, dreaming of bigger things, to forget how small we are.

I am atheism, and all that I am belongs to you, so live, love, err, adventure, learn, and never apologize to the sky.

Acknowledgements

My grandmother, Eleanor, always showed me that life is at its best when you're having fun with it and not taking things so seriously. For someone like me who is naturally serious, her personality and enjoyment of people and life taught me how to give myself a counterweight that I needed. I love you, Grandma.

My friend, Kris Lecki, happened to take his trip of religious extraction in parallel with me, and since this is likely the last book I will write on the subject, I wanted to acknowledge the support that that gave me as I withdrew from the ideology. I'm proud to call you a friend.

There are many people who have given my first work exceptional support, far beyond what I could have fairly expected, and I acknowledge them here in alphabetical order: Thomas Beisheim; Robert Copley; Joshua Ghiringhelli; Shea King; John Langston; Alesha Lauri; Andi Lee; Simona Longoni; Joshua Osmun; Jeff Peterson; Kevin Steward; Chris Stewart; Raye Sutton; David Viviano. I am grateful to you all, and I hope you bond with and love this project just as much.

About the Author

Christopher Krzeminski is 31 years old. He holds a B.A. in Mathematics from Duke University in Durham, NC and a J.D. from The University of Alabama School of Law in Tuscaloosa, AL. He currently resides in New Jersey.

He may be contacted for questions or comments by email at chris.krzeminski1@gmail.com or on Twitter @marco_iO9 where he writes under the pseudonym, Marco the Atheist.

www.ingramcontent.com/pod-product-compliance
Lightning Source LLC
Chambersburg PA
CBHW020507030426
42337CB00011B/262